questions

questions

questions

questions

questions

questions

questions

questions

questions

questions

questions

questions

questions

The Phil**?**osophers' Club

ILLUSTRATED BY

KIM DONER

WRITTEN BY

CHRISTOPHER PHILLIPS

Tricycle Press

Berkeley | Toronto

Welcome to the Philosophers' Club

No one questions, no one wonders, no one examines, like children. It is not simply that children love questions, but that they *live* questions. Most children are young versions of that quintessential questioner from ancient Athens—namely, Socrates. The 5th century B.C. philosopher cultivated his childlike, but by no means childish, questioning nature throughout his life by engaging in what we now call "Socratic dialogues."

A Socratic dialogue is simply a way of questioning that inspires people to come up with their own answers, to find truth by their own lights. The form of Socratic dialogue I practice does not have any specific answer as the goal. It's the *questioning* that is important.

One of the greatest issues today in education is why our children often do not seem to think for themselves. Children who take part regularly in Socratic dialogues develop and hone critical and creative thinking skills which will help them become more autonomous individuals. They learn to make well-reasoned decisions. Most of all, they are better able to ask and answer those most important of questions, "Who am I?" and "Who can I become?" This book models Socratic dialogues for children, and shows that engaging in Socratic dialogues is not just something to be reserved for school time. This way of questioning can be done anytime, anywhere, and can easily become a way of life.

I and other educators and adults who engage in Socratic dialogues with children on a regular basis have found again and again that children of all learning levels, and of all social and economic backgrounds, excel in the "fourth R"—the ability to reason. Children who take part in Socratic dialogues use this ability in breathtakingly imaginative and constructive ways. (Many of the questions asked in this book came from children I've worked with.) Their sense of self is strengthened, and as a result, they're more motivated to develop their abilities in the traditional three Rs.

Try reading aloud one of the dialogues (which you'll find complete on double-page spreads) with a single child or a group, then ask one of the questions on the page that follows. You can also request a free readers' guide by mailing a #10 SASE with two first-class stamps to the publisher or download it from www.tenspeed.com.

It's critical for adults to engage in Socratic dialogues with children—during school hours and afterward, at home and at youth centers. Doing so opens up pathways of communication between kids and adults that other forms of dialogue simply do not. They talk to one another on an equal level, each gaining insights from the other. And it is one great way to help children become more tolerant and thoughtful critical thinkers. Why not help children you know start a Philosophers' Club today?

—Christopher Phillips, 2001

Questions

Which came first, the chicken or the egg?

What is philosophy?

What is violence?

Is this glass half empty or half full?

Is it possible to be happy and sad at the same time?

What is silence?

Why do we ask questions?

What is the difference between the truth and a lie?

Are the mind and the brain the same thing?

Why are we here?

"Which came first, the chicken or the egg?"

Why does one of them have to come first?

Because all chickens have been hatched from eggs.

Then the egg came first! But where did it come from?

I think it's made of "pre-egg" parts that somehow came to form the egg.

And where did the parts come from in the first place?

Where did anything come from?

questions questions questions

What is "first"?

Was there a first chicken? A first egg? A first kiss?
A first first? A last first? A first last?

Is there a last to go with every first?

Is every first different from every other first?

Is every new moment a first?

Is every first a beginning? Is every last an ending?

Is the moment in which a chicken hatches from an egg
both a beginning and an ending?

"What is philosophy?"

Philosophy is the study of "Why?"

It's finding the answer to "Who am I?" and "Why am I?" and "Where am I?"

Philosophy is also an ancient Greek word that means "love of wisdom."

What is wisdom?

Wisdom is what you get as you learn and know more about yourself and the world around you.

But there's always more and more to know.

How could you ever know if you knew all there is to know?

questions questions questions

How can you love wisdom?

Is there such a thing as bad wisdom?

Do you know a wise person?
If so, how do you know if he or she is wise?

Is it possible to hate wisdom?

Is there a difference between knowing
and learning?

How can you use what you know
in good ways?

What do questions have to do
with philosophy?

How do you know when you know something?

"What is violence?"

Violence is someone hurting someone else or something on purpose.

But what about when two planets collide and destroy each other?

Yeah. They didn't mean to do it.

Violence is always hurting something, but it's not always bad.

I kill germs when I wash my hands with hot water and soap.

That's good violence, because it keeps you from getting sick.

It seems like violence always changes things.

Is change a kind of violence?

questions questions questions

What is change?

Does violence always do harm?

If two planets collide, and no one's there
to see it happen, has violence occurred?

Can colors be violent?

Is disrespect a form of violence?

Is love violent?

Can you do violence to something
that isn't alive? Can something that isn't alive
do violence to you?

What would our world be like without violence?

Are questions violent?

"Is this glass half empty or half full?"

It's half empty of water *and* half empty of air.

It's half full of water and half empty of water.

No, it's half empty of water and half full of air.

It's completely full of water and air.

But it's completely empty of lots of things, too.

It's empty of everything except water and air.

What about the surface, where the water and the air meet?

Is the surface empty or full…or both…or neither?

questions questions questions

What is empty? What is full?

For something to be empty or full,
does it have to have limits or boundaries?

Is the universe empty or full?

Is a human being in any way empty or full?

Is there any such thing as completely empty or full?

What does it mean to live "a full life" or "an empty life"?

Can you be full of emptiness?

Is empty the same as nothing?

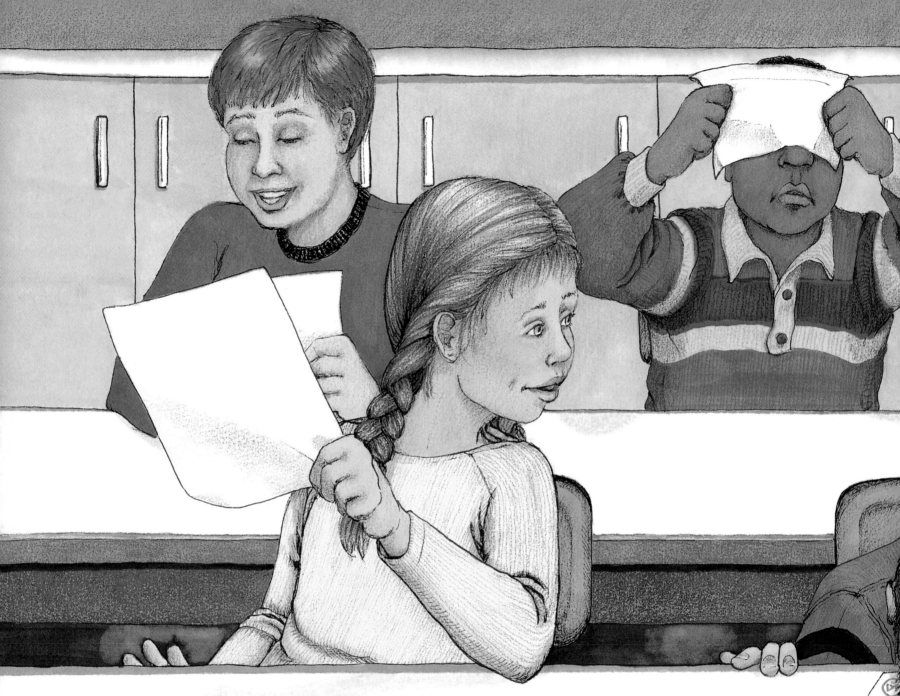

"Is it possible to be happy and sad at the same time?"

Sure. I'm happy whenever my family goes to visit my grandmother over the summer, but sad that I leave behind all my friends.

I'm happy that I'm growing older, but I'm sad that my parents are.

I was sad when my cousin died, but I'm happy he's not suffering anymore.

I'm happy when I ask questions…but I'm miserable too, because there never seems to be a final answer.

So it's a happy kind of miserable, isn't it?

Would you even know "happy" if you didn't know "sad" too?

questions questions questions

What are emotions?

Can you create new emotions?

Can you decide which emotions you'll have
and which you won't have?

What is happy? What is sad?

How do you know when you're happy or sad?

Where do happy and sad come from?

Is it possible to be completely happy or completely sad?

Is sad the opposite of happy?
Is angry the opposite of happy?

Is there a difference between joy and happiness?
Between sadness and depression?

Can you be sad to be happy or happy to be sad?

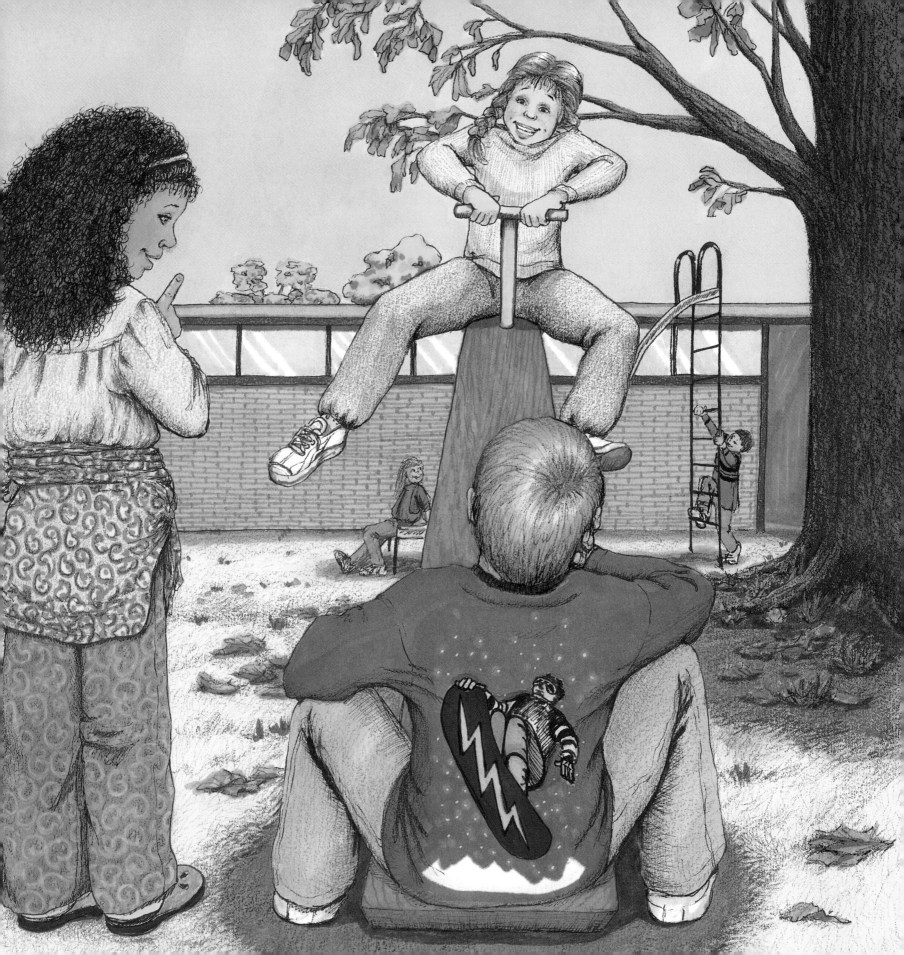

"What is silence?"

If there's no noise, there's silence.

But thinking thoughts isn't silence, even though there's no noise.

Yeah, thoughts are voices inside your head, and voices aren't silent.

So there's never complete silence, even if you don't make any noise.

Right, because I can't turn off the voices in my head.

Hmmmm...is silence just a special kind of noise?

questions questions questions

What is noise?

Can some thoughts be completely silent?

How do you know when you're thinking?

Are there different kinds of thinking?

Is listening a kind of silence?

Can you talk and listen at the same time?

Is listening the same as hearing?

Can you hear someone else if you're not silent?

Can you hear yourself if you're not silent?

What is the opposite of silence?

"Why do we ask questions?"

Because we wonder.

Because we're curious.

Because something has happened that
we don't understand.

Some people just ask questions they know the answer to.

> Do you mean like, when I ask a friend, "Do you like my new bike?" and I already think she'll say, "Yes"?

Right. But what if she surprises you and says, "No"?

> Hmmm…maybe we ask questions to see if the answer we get is the one we think we'll get.

So, do we ask questions to discover if we really know what we think we know?

questions questions questions

What would life be like without questions?

Can you ask a question about something
you know nothing about?

Can a question be an answer?
Can an answer be a question?

Is there ever a final answer to any question?

How do you know when you've
answered a question?

Is it possible to be too curious?

Why do you ask questions?

What do you think is the most
important question you can ask?

"What is the difference between the truth and a lie?"

The truth is good and a lie is bad.

Not always! If I were hiding a runaway slave during the days of slavery, and some-one trying to catch him asked me if he was in my house, I'd say, "No."

So sometimes a lie can be good?

Sometimes, but almost always it's best to be honest.

Is truth the same as honesty?

If I'm going to be honest, then I need to make sure the truth is really the truth.

But do you ever know the truth once and for all?

questions questions questions

What is belief?

Is there a difference between a true belief
and a false one?

Can something be false without being a lie?

Can you honestly lie?

Can you lie without meaning to do so?

Is there a difference between a lie
and a fib?

What is a half-truth?

Is there such a thing as
"the whole truth"?

"Are the mind and the brain the same thing?"

No, the brain is inside your body, but your mind is everywhere.

I think the brain is the mind's home.

Without the mind, we wouldn't even know we had a brain!

The mind tells the brain what to do, and then the brain makes the rest of the body follow the mind's orders.

Does your mind make your brain go to sleep at night?

How can your brain be asleep if you dream while you're sleeping?

Your brain and mind are still awake while you're asleep.

Does that mean they don't belong to me?

When I dream, is the mind in my dream awake, even if my real mind is asleep?

Are we dreaming right now?

questions questions questions

Are humans the only beings with minds?

What is your real mind?

Can you touch your mind?

If your mind is everywhere,
where is everywhere?

If your mind is in your brain,
where in your brain is it?

Is your mind also in your heart?

If your mind tells your brain what to do,
how does it
go about doing this?

Can you have a brain without a mind?
A mind without a brain?

Is it possible not to use your mind?

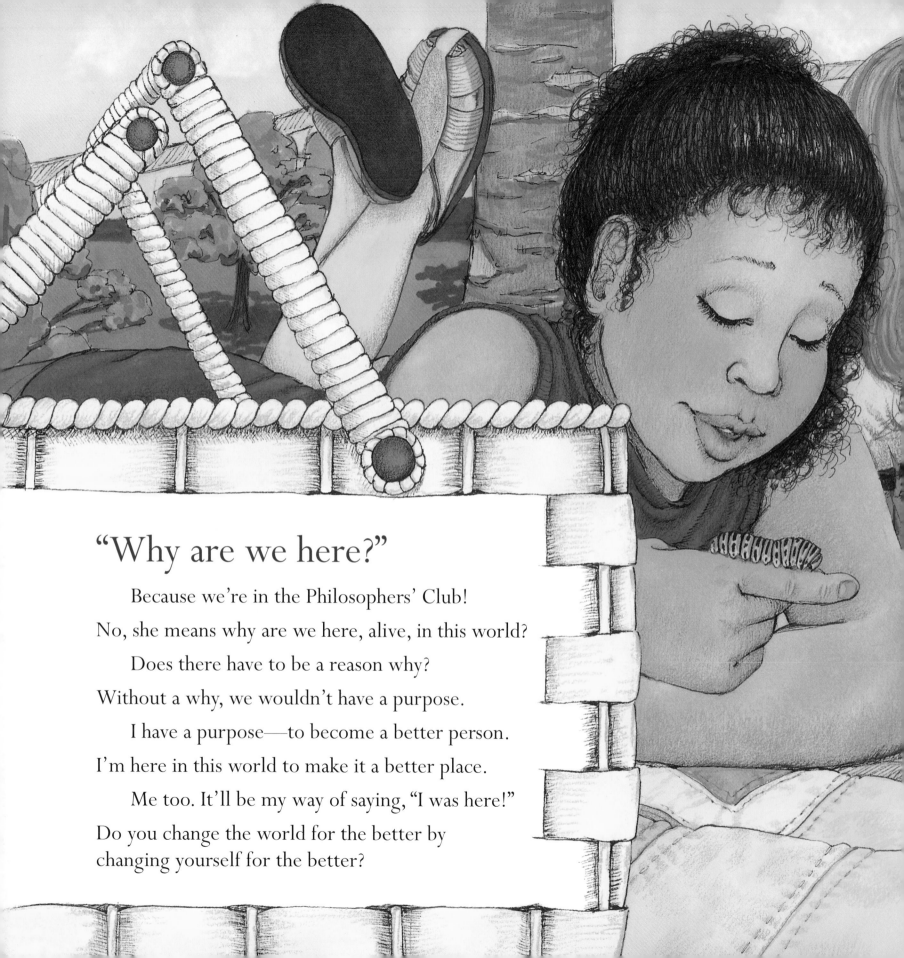

"Why are we here?"

Because we're in the Philosophers' Club!

No, she means why are we here, alive, in this world?

Does there have to be a reason why?

Without a why, we wouldn't have a purpose.

I have a purpose—to become a better person.

I'm here in this world to make it a better place.

Me too. It'll be my way of saying, "I was here!"

Do you change the world for the better by
changing yourself for the better?

questions questions questions

What is here? When is here? Where is here?

Would you know if you weren't here?

Do you have to be here?

Are there other heres besides this here?

Is there a difference between a reason
and a purpose?

Is nowhere a type of here?

Is there a difference between responsibility
and obligation?

How do you know whether the world
has become a better place?

For Cecilia, and for the childlike,
but by no means childish,
questioner within us all —C.P.

For all the kids who are
brave enough to ask. —K.D.

Tricycle Press
A little division of Ten Speed Press
P.O. Box 7123
Berkeley, California 94707
www.tenspeed.com

Book design by Frances Soo Ping Chow
Typeset in Perpetua and Caslon Open Face

Library of Congress Cataloging-in-Publication Data

Phillips, Christopher, 1959 July 15–
       The philosophers' club / Christopher Phillips ; illustrations by Kim Doner.
          p. cm.
       Contents: What is philosophy? — What is a question? — Are the mind and
the brain the same thing? — Is this glass half empty or half full? — Is it possible to
be happy and sad at the same time? — What is silence? — What is violence? —
Which came first, the chicken or the egg? — What is the difference between the
truth and a lie? — Why are we here?
     ISBN 1-58246-039-6
     1. Philosophy—Juvenile literature. [1. Philosophy.] I. Doner, Kim, 1955– ill.
II. Title.
BD31 .P55 2001
100—dc21   00–010662

First printing, 2001
Printed in China

1 2 3 4 5 6 7 — 05 04 03 02 01

questions

questions

questions

questions

questions

questions

questions

JUL 2000

Northport-East Northport Public Library

To view your patron record from a computer, click on
the Library's homepage: **www.nenpl.org**

You may:
- request an item be placed on hold
- renew an item that is overdue
- view titles and due dates checked out on your card
- view your own outstanding fines

**151 Laurel Avenue
Northport, NY 11768
631-261-6930**